FLIGHT

Written by Alexander Barrie
Illustrated by Geoff Pleasance

© 1994 Henderson Publishing Limited

Henderson

Woodbridge, England *Publishing*

FLYING AND FLAPPING

Fiery Flight

Jacques-Etienne Montgolfier made the first passenger-carrying hot air balloon - but wisely never flew in it himself. Instead, a science teacher named Jean Pilétre de Rozier and an army officer, the Marquis d'Arlandes, did so in November 1783. They ran amazing risks shovelling straw into an open fire under the huge cotton and paper balloon. The balloon itself caught fire several times and the daring men doused it with spongefuls of water. They nearly crashed in central Paris but managed to land safely in parkland. They had flown for 25 minutes - to become the world's first aviators.

Flapping Leonardo

As anyone might guess the brilliant Leonardo da Vinci was the first to dream seriously about flying. He thought it would have to be done by flapping wings. In 1490 he designed an extraordinary machine with turning handles, pulleys and foot pedals to flap wings made of netting covered with feathers. He probably never built his design and certainly didn't try to fly it. Many other hopefuls jumped from high places flapping home made wings - all fell to the ground and most died.

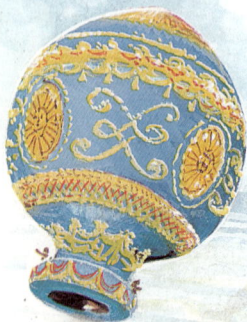

I Don't Mind

Centuries after Leonardo's time, inventors were still trying to fly like the birds - though nobody seemed to think of including one important detail - the bird's tail. One of the last, and most persistent of the birdmen, was E P Frost. He was still flapping giant crow-like feather-covered wings when real flight began. Frost knew then that he had got it wrong but said, 'I don't begrudge the time and trouble I've expended.'

Why Didn't They See?

If the wing flappers had looked around they would have seen gliders doing better. In 1853 a British engineer, Sir George Caley, built a glider that looked remarkably modern with up-tilted monoplane (single) wings. Sir George was 80, so made his chauffeur fly in the machine across a Yorkshire valley. After the flight the frightened chauffeur resigned!

Gliders Crashed Too

A German engineer, Otto Lilienthal, was a brilliant glider designer and flier. He understood that there was a lot to learn about piloting before putting in a heavy engine. In 1896, after making more than 2,000 successful flights, he lost control, said 'Sacrifices must be made' - and died.

GETTING IT RIGHT

Wright You Are

Two American brothers, Orville and Wilbur Wright, achieved the first true powered flight. Their petrol engined aircraft, neatly named the 'Flyer', lived up to its name in December 1903, and flew for 12 seconds at 48 kph, piloted by Orville. The Wrights made three more flights that day in North Carolina but wrecked the aeroplane. Only two years later they were flying for 30 minutes and more. Few people cared.

First in Britain

And an American, Samuel Cody, was the first man to build and fly an aircraft in Britain. He built an aircraft for the British army known as 'British Army Aeroplane No 1'. It had one engine and two propellers, and first flew in 1908.

Curves for Lift

It was well understood by now that when air streamed over a curved wing the top surface would be 'sucked' upwards and the underside would be pushed up from below, giving lift.

Blériot Channel Hops

In 1909, just a year after Cody's flight, Louis Blériot, a Frenchman, flew the Channel to win a newspaper prize. He travelled 41.8 km from Calais in 36 minutes and landed heavily in Dover. He is reported to have said, simply, 'Mon Dieu!'. He'd flown in a monoplane.

How Many Wings?

Blériot's aeroplane, with the dull name Type XI, was surprisingly modern with a rudder for turning, and elevators on the tail plane for climbing or diving and a sprung undercarriage. Blériot didn't know about ailerons (hinged flaps on the trailing edges of wings) to make the plane bank. But he'd learned from the Wright brothers how to get the same effect by twisting the wings by pulling wires.

Warplane aerobatics

The Great War of 1914/18 brought aircraft design forward fast. The stubby-winged biplane was most favoured - though the German Fokker triplane (three sets of wings) had some success. The great Baron von Richthoven, the 'Red Baron', made some of his 80 'kills' in the red coloured triplane. Dog fights called for daring aerobatics. Aircraft became strong and reliable, and pilot skills very high. Ailerons arrived for steep banks.

Bombers for Peace

Heavy bombers, biplanes again, were rapidly developed in 1914/18 too, including the huge four-engined Handley Page V/1500. After the war, bombers could be converted to carry passengers. Perhaps the bomber to win most fame for a peaceful mission was the twin Rolls-Royce engined Vickers Vimy. In June 1919, a Vimy made the first non-stop Atlantic crossing crewed by Capt John Alcock and Lt Arthur Brown. The crossing took 16 hours 27 minutes and Alcock and Brown had to sit in an icy cold open cockpit. They had little more than a compass, altimeter and clock to help them.

Goliath the Gentle

The square and ugly Farman Goliath was another twin engined bomber put to peaceful use in about 1920. There was a passenger cabin in the front and another amidships. The unfortunate pilot sat in an open cockpit between the cabins. The Goliath's speed was only 150 kph, but 60 were sold.

Making a Mistake

The American Curtiss Company was slow to see that converting bombers to carry passengers would be short term. In the 1920s the company offered its twin-engined biplane bomber, the Condor 11, as a 12-passenger airliner. The Condor was quite fast at 240 kph and had the good range of 1,150 km. Few went into service - the scene was changing.

Another Oddity

Other out of date airliners survived better - like the de Havilland DH 86 four engined biplane built of wood and fabric. It appeared as late as 1934, carrying 10 passengers at 142 mph as far as 800 miles. A smaller twin engine version, the 89A 'Rapide', was also successful despite carrying only 8 passengers and having a one-man cockpit so small that some people said they needed twelve-year-old pilots.

No Thanks - I'll Swim

The first of daily flights from London to Paris was on 25th August 1919 with a single passenger. It could be a hairy adventure. One pilot took two days for the two-hour journey and had 33 mini crashes on the way.

Your Captain Speaking

Three British 'airlines' fought it out on the Paris run. One was a shipping company - it started calling its pilots captains and other airlines followed..

Lonely Crossing

People were astonished when a dashing young American flier, Charles Lindbergh, nicknamed 'Lucky Lindy', made the first solo flight across the Atlantic in 1927. It took him 33 hr 29 min to cover the distance of 5,810 km from Long Island, New York, to Le Bourgeot, Paris. There was no automatic pilot in those days, and he said that towards the end he didn't know whether he was awake or asleep. Once he woke up in darkness to find the aeroplane flying on its side. His aircraft, a monoplane, named Spirit of St. Louis, is preserved in the Smithsonian Institution. Atlantic hopping was about to become possible for everyone.

New Idea - Metal

One of the most remarkable feats in aviation history came as early as 1919 when Germany produced the all-metal, monoplane Junkers F13 for Lufthansa. Described as an airliner, though it only carried four passengers, it was the first all metal aeroplane to fly commercially. At first the pilot and observer sat in an open cockpit - but this was soon closed in. It had a corrugated skin which was very strong and looked stylish. The F13, years ahead of its time, was to lead to bigger, faster all-metal airliners.

Tomorrow Today

By 1933 two major American aircraft companies were developing models that, as one expert puts it today, 'Clearly marked the birth of the modern airliner.' Britain was being left sadly behind.

The Boeing 247

Although America's Boeing 247 flew first in 1933 it looks quite modern even today - an all-metal low wing monoplane with retracting gear and streamlined engine cowlings. Its payload was small - 10 passengers, but they travelled in comfort at 305 kph. Range: 1,200 km.

Famed Dakota DC-3

Like Boeing, Douglas flew a fine new aircraft in 1933 - another all-metal monoplane. This was the DC-1, which was quickly improved to become the DC-2 - then the world famous DC-3, usually called the Dakota. DC-3s continued in production throughout and beyond the war. Many thousands of them were built for military and passenger use, and some are still flying. The range was vast for its day - 3,420 km at 333 kph. A flying workhorse if ever there was one.

Slow but Safe for Britain

Britain's aircraft manufacturing industry was losing the race against American technology. Britain produced stately aircraft like the Handley Page H.P.42 Horatius flown by Imperial Airways. It was an old fashioned 160 kph, twin engined biplane which could cover 805 km. At least Handley Page had an unbeaten record for safety.

DODGY GIANTS

Risky Airships

Dirigibles (the fancy word for airships) have a long up and down history - in more ways than one. The first was flown in 1852 when Frenchman, Henri Giffard made one and powered it with a heavy and dangerous steam engine. It was 43.8 m long, flew a short distance - and was more or less useless.

Count von Zeppelin Does Better

The Germans took up airship design, and made petrol engined zeppelins, named after the Count who inspired them. Between 1910 and 1914 they were remarkably successful, carrying 35,000 passengers safely. During the war, zeppelins were used to drop bombs on England.

The Flying 'Graf'

After the war, zeppelins returned to passenger carrying. One, the Graf Zeppelin ('graf' is German for count) flew for nine busy years, from 1928 till 1937, covering an astonishing 1,250,000 miles without a single accident.

Flammable Gas

The trouble with airships was in the gas that took them up. It was hydrogen, made from sulphuric acid dripped on iron, and highly flammable.

Disaster

After so many successful years, disasters struck time and again. Two huge dirigibles were made in Britain - the R100 and R101. They took passengers over long, slow distances, including across the Atlantic. Experts saw a dazzling future for airship travel. But in 1930, the R101 caught fire on its first flight as it arrived at its mooring post, and all 50 passengers died horribly.

And more disasters

Just as confidence in airship travel was returning, two American machines crashed. They were the Shenandoah and Akron which came to grief in 1933. In 1937, even the Germans came unstuck when their enormous Hindenberg went down to destruction. And Germany had seen about 30 other airships crash. So many lives had been lost that confidence was lost too, almost for good.

One of the First

The world's biggest airline used to be Pan Am, of the USA. In 1928, aware that there were few airfields but unlimited water surfaces it began to fly an 'amphibian', an aircraft that could be based on land or sea. The Sikorsky S-38 biplane with floats and wheels went into service, carrying 10 passengers at 165 kph. It could travel 800 km in one hop. Other airlines quickly took up the idea.

Big but Limited

Within two years Pan Am began operating a large 4-engined Sikorsky flying boat, the S-40. It could carry what then seemed a very large number of passengers, 40, at 185 kph. But there was a snag - its range was only 50 miles. And it had no wheels - it had to find water to land on or crash!

Still the Leaders

Boeing and Pan Am achieved another 'first' in 1938 when their regular trans-Atlantic flights began. The service was named Yankee Clipper. Boeing's 314 flying boat, then the world's biggest aircraft, flew 77 passengers non-stop from New York to Southampton at 280 kph.

Short - and Great

The British company Short made some of the finest
flying boats ever seen. As early as 1928 they
produced the S.8 Calcutta, a 3-engined biplane,
the first to have an all-metal 'stressed' skin.
They were marvellously
trouble-free, and in
service with Imperial
Airways. They
cruised at about
160 kph for
as far as
1,050 km.

C Class Wonders

Even today most people would recognise the shape
of the rugged-looking Short C class flying boats.
Here was a technological milestone - all metal
built, with flaps that were electrically powered and
propellers that could change their pitch (roughly
meaning the amount of twist in them). The first to
fly was named Canopus. There were some bad
crashes, but the C class were truly global, linking
Britain and Australia, and carrying 24 passengers.

Short's Giant G

The G looked like the C flying boat but was much
bigger. Just as it was about to start regular trans-
Atlantic flights in 1939 the war started, which
ended that. The G had a huge range, 5,150 km,
and was used by the RAF as the famous
Sunderland.

Flying Flea

In about 1934, a Frenchman, Henri Mignet, designed and built a tiny motorcycle engined aeroplane, called the Sky Louse. He decided to bring it to Britain in 1935, now named the Flying Flea. He was not a good pilot. Mignet paused at Calais before crossing the Channel - and crashed the Flea, which was not unusual for him. He made quick repairs, tied an inflated bike inner tube round his waist, and flew on over the sea, this time landing right way up. He said the Flea was cheap, and easy to build and fly. The DIY aeroplane caused a sensation. But there was crash after crash. Soon the Flying Fleas were banned. Owners sadly broke them up for firewood.

Don't Look Back

The Caudron GIII had a strange design dating back to 1912. It was a kind of flying shoe for two, with the stubby shoe of a cockpit set in an alarmingly open tube framework. The man in the rear needed specially good nerves - there was almost nothing behind him. It cruised at 90 kph. The Caudron last flew in 1936 and can be seen today in a museum.

Guppy? Or Whale?

One of the strangest looking aircraft, a transporter, is the Guppy, often called the Pregnant Guppy. Its open interior is enormous. The freight compartment is 6.2 m high by 5.08 m. It can cruise at 410 kph.

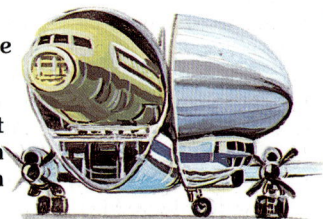

What a Waste

American Howard Hughes was a rich and extraordinary man, a film maker, business tycoon and pilot. He largely designed and built, then flew an enormous eight-engined flying boat named Spruce Goose. It weighed nearly 200 tonnes. The whole journey was barely more than half a mile, and it was the only flight the huge machine ever made.

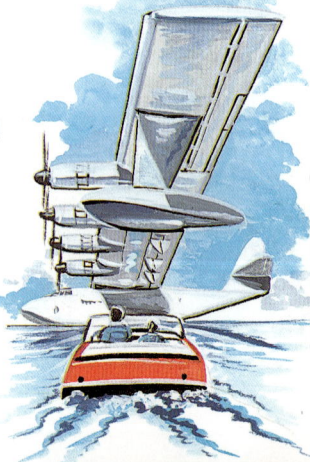

Upward Thrust

The search for Vertical Take Off and Landing aircraft has produced some odd sights. The 1968 French designed Nord 500 with its huge engines, upwards facing at take off, was stranger than most. It should have had a speed of 350 kph but was not a success.

Keeping Warm

The de Havilland company cashed in on earlier success with the Gipsy Moth by producing a snug cabin tourer, in 1930, the D.H.80 Puss Moth. This was a genuine tourer with seating for three people and room for baggage. They also turned the engine upside down which reduced drag. And they made the fuselage structure of steel tube for strength. Highest speed was 210 kph and range 725 km.

And the Tiger

The D.H.82 Tiger Moth was aptly named, a tiger indeed, and highly aerobatic. Many pilots found themselves upside down for the first time in a Tiger's open cockpit, and never forgot the moment. Speed, 167 kph, range 480 km.

Getting Modern

After the second world war US constructors cornered the private plane market, with the French coming second. Again Britain lagged. Cessna were one of the most successful US light aircraft builders, with their high wing single engined monoplanes. The type 150 did spectacularly well. So did the beefed up aerobatic version, the Aerobat.

surprised to be sued by the widow of a man who bought one of their aircraft and killed himself by crashing it. The widow claimed the company should not have let him buy it - and won!

Beech Too

A third major American manufacturer was Beech. Their single engined Musketeer did well. It had retractable gear and could be used for touring or sporty aerobatics. Cruise speed was 255 kph, range, 1,272 km.

Piper Are Sued

Another big American name in aircraft manufacturing is Piper. Perhaps their best known light plane, first seen in 1960, was the Cherokee, a low wing single engined 3 to 4 seater with elegantly spatted landing wheels. It could cruise at 330 kph, travelling 1,665 km. Piper were

French Version

French manufacturers kept pressure on the US. The Socata Rallye, 1966, a one engine 4-seater was jeered at by some, 'The French apology for an aircraft', some would say. But it was a popular low wing monoplane and, unlike many other single engined planes, had retracting gear and was quite fast at 275 kph. Also it had a range of nearly 1,130 km - so why the scoffing?

Cheeky Chipmunk

The British took the Canadian built de Havilland Chipmunk to its heart. A single engined 2-seater, one man behind the other, it had a fighter plane type sliding canopy, and was highly aerobatic. Its general perfomance wasn't exactly great - speed 235 kph, range, 780 kph. But the Chipmunk was fun.

High Performance

Another popular French light aircraft was the Jodel, a 3-seater, by Pierre Robin. It had cranked up wingtips, and was considered sporty - but with a top speed of 215 kph was it so special? The range, 1,250 km was good.

Nippy Twins

In the 60s some smart, comfortable, fast and reliable twin engined, light monoplane aircraft began to appear. Predictably, most were American - like the Piper Aztec. The Aztec came in various versions, each new model showing improvements. The Aztec F could carry six people (and their baggage) in comfort cruising at 338 kph non-stop for 2,445 km. They had autopilot, and advanced navigation and radio aids.

And Cessna's 310

Piper's main competitor, Cessna, were in the market place with their popular twin engined 310 series, and other models. Later 310s had pressurised cabins and turbocharged engines and, at a pinch, could carry six people. It was not as fast as the Aztec at 255 kph but its range was impressively greater at 2,840 km. Some carried cargo. One 310 often carried thousands of two-day old chicks as passengers. Their tiny bodies stoked up so much heat that special air cooling of the cabin was needed.

HELICOPTERS

Leonardo First Again
The astonishing Leonardo left more than 500 sketches and 35,000 words on flight. Needless to say he thought of helicopters all those centuries ago and sketched one.

Up and Forward
Many engineers over many years thought about the idea of 'rotating wings' (blades). The problem was how to get lift with forward travel. In 1923, a Spaniard, Juan de la Cierva, made the first flight by autogyro. He had a free spinning rotor overhead, and an engine driven propellor in front. He realised that the forward motion of the aircraft would spin the rotor and give lift. It was really an aeroplane without fixed wings - not a true helicopter. Cierva's C4 autogyro caused huge excitement. He improved his machines year by year, flying one of them across the Channel at 160 kph. By the 1930s his C30 model was seen as replacing cars. That didn't happen.

Feeling Dizzy

The big problem with the helicopter idea was 'torque' - when the powered overhead rotor spun one way, the body of the aircraft spun the other. Igor Sikorsky, a Russian aircraft engineer who had settled in the US, solved the torque snag with his R4 helicopter design of 1939. He simply fitted a small propeller - or rotor - to the tail. It resisted the turning effect, and the true helicopter had been born. The US army realized its potential at once.

More War and Peace

Helicopters are widely used by armed forces all over the world. But their peaceful uses are many. One of Sikorsky's recent helicopters is the S-76 Spirit. It has an elegant almost delicate appearance but is a great worker. The Spirit has a cruising speed of 285 kph - fast for such machines - and can carry two pilots and 12 passengers. Its first flight was 1977.

Tilt the Rotor

Helicopters climb, dive, hover, turn right or left simply by tilting the overhead rotor. Even so they are surprisingly difficult to fly.

Boeing Again

The world's biggest aircraft manufacturer, Boeing, also make the world's biggest capacity helicopter, the 234 Chinook. It has twin rotors and can carry 44 passengers and two pilots. There is a military version often used as a gunship. The Chinook cruises at 270 kph, and can cover 1,064 km non-stop.

Search and Rescue

The Westland Sea King is best known for its humanitarian work finding and rescuing people in danger. It has a large carrying capacity and its bright yellow shape is often seen on TV hovering over stormy waves or cliff ledges while the winch man is lowered to haul somebody up to the safety of the cabin. Operated by the RAF it can reach 230 kph with the useful range of 1,230 km.

Years Ahead

The Americans were years ahead of everyone else in the building of long-haul aircraft during the post war years. In 1949, Pan Am took the lead again by flying Boeing Stratocruisers across the Atalantic. It had double-deck pressurised cabins, and passengers were amazed at the space and comfort offered them. The aircraft could reach 600 kph - fast! It was developed from the Superfortress bomber, and was good for 6,760 km.

piston engined aircraft were carrying a million people a year across the Atlantic.

Willing Viscount

One British achievement was production of the first successful turbo-prop 4-engined plane, the Vickers Viscount. It was constantly improved through the '50s and was much admired. The Viscount could carry 70 passengers, cruised at 560 kph with a range of 2,735 km. The Viscount still flies.

Made for the Job

One of the first big aircraft specially built for carrying passengers was the beautiful Lockheed Super Constellation - or 'Connie'. Holland's KLM airline were first to use it. Soon large

Whispering Giant

Another British success in the '50s was the elegant Bristol Britannia, a huge four engined turbo-prop so quiet that it was nicknamed the Whispering Giant. It could carry 100 passengers and with the big range of 9,260 km, flew regularly non-stop from London to New York. It cruised at 580 kph.

Russia Too

Russia, which had been lagging in the design of big airliners, did a lot to catch up in the '60s by producing the Ilyushin. It had four of the latest turbo-prop engines and was amazingly fast at about 675 kph. It was a good load carrier too - about 120 passengers could fly non-stop for over 6,450 km.

Nice to be Rich

During the '60s and '70s many fine aircraft were produced for executive travel for the rich and for carrying people short distances. They were pressurised, so could fly at high altitudes and many were turbo-prop powered. In turbo-prop engines, hot gases are made to spin a turbine instead of driving pistons up and down. Beech's King Air 100 was an early success - in the mid '60s it appeared with twin turbo-prop engines and a seating capacity of 15. As usual, improvements were made and, renamed as the 200, it was in much demand, cruising at 525 kph for 3,750 km.

Cessna Again

One of the US 'biggies', Cessna, announced their first turbo-prop twin in 1977, named the Conquest. It crashed and needed some redesigning, but became a success, though slower than some, cruising at 480 kph.

Fast Climb

The 4 engined de Havilland Dash 7 has slotted wings that let it take off after a short run, then climb quickly and quietly. It carries 50, at 420 kph, for about 1,280 km.

Turbojets Arrive
Britain's Sir Frank Whittle was one of two pioneer inventors of the turbojet engine. As early as 1937 the Whittle engine was test run - a true turbojet. A fuel and air mix was compressed and burnt and blasted out of the rear of the engine to create a forward reaction. The Germans flew a jet engined aircraft first - the Heinkel He 178. But Whittle soon followed with his Gloster E 28/39 powered by a single engine which first flew in 1941. Pistons and even propellers were becoming old hat. The Gloster had a top speed of 565 kph - not very fast yet, though full of promise. But Whittle lost control of his invention.

Twins
While the twin jet engined Gloster Meteor was still being developed the Germans got ahead again with their Messerschmitt Me 262 - also a jet twin, which flew in 1944. And the 262 was faster - capable of 870 kph. But after the war it was Whittle's engine that aeroplane constructors decided to take up, the US and Russia included.

Jet Disaster

There are no motorway limits for aircraft, and high speed has always been the aim. The British de Havilland company and America's Boeing were two rivals out to produce the first large, long range, near speed-of-sound passenger jets. De Havilland's 4-jet Comet, a beautiful aircraft, flew first, in 1952, starting a regular trans-Atlantic service. But one of the saddest episodes in aviation history was to follow. Two of the aircraft crashed, killing everyone on board. The Comet service was withdrawn in 1954. In an astonishing experiment a surviving Comet was put in a vast water tank and hydraulically stressed. Metal fatigue soon showed. Part of the cause was that the engines were set into the wings instead of under them, causing weakness in the structure. A strengthened Comet 4 flew successfully with the RAF from 1958. But it had been a bitter blow for British aviation.

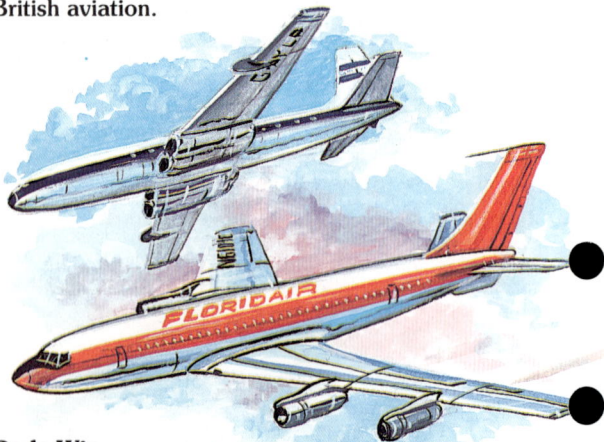

Pods Win

Boeing chose (correctly) to hang the engines on pods under the aircraft's wings. Their 4-engined 707 flew in 1954, best speed: 975kph. Range, 5,834 km. The 707 was smoky but highly successful, and was used by most major airlines.

A French First

French plane builders Sud-Est quickly followed the 707 with their handsome Caravelle which flew in 1954. It had two rear-mounted jet engines and was the first short range jetliner. It could cruise at 805 kph, with 80 passengers, for 1,690 km.

Britain's VC10

The British company, Vickers, also made a rear engined jet - but chose 4 engines for their VC10, and a very high tail. The aircraft was good at coping with 'thin' hot or high air, but wasn't a big sales success, though the RAF liked the VC10 and fitted the seats, 150 of them, so that passengers faced backwards - known to be safer. The range was good - over 8,000 km.

One-Elevens Everywhere

The British-made One-Eleven, by BAC, has been seen in action widely since the mid '60s. It is a twin rear-engined, high tailed plane, of medium range, carrying 119 people at 870 kph. Worthy.

SPEED – THE ARGUMENT

Faster Still

The quest for speed continued and together BAC of Britain and Aerospatiale of France decided to build an airliner that could break through the 'sound barrier' - go faster than sound itself, which travels at about 1,220 kph. That had been done as long before as 1947, and since, but by small military aircraft. Supersonic speeds are measured in 'Mach' units. To go beyond Mach 1 (speed of sound) and maintain the speed with a large airliner, raised daunting technical difficulties. It cost British and French taxpayers more than £2 billion to overcome them. The aeroplane was first known, boringly, as SST. There was much argument about a better name - then the young son of a BAC boss suggested Concorde. It stuck. Concorde has been flying since 1969, carries 100 passengers, cruises at Mach 2.2, and can cover 6,440 km. It stretches 25 cm in flight. Noise limit rules have been bent for Concorde as for no other aircraft - like for take-off. At its very high cruising speed it makes a mighty 'sonic boom', so has to slow down over land to prevent it. Even so it can fly from New York to London in 2 hr 55 min.

Not For Us

The major US aircraft builders steered well clear of supersonics believing Concorde would never make money. They were right for years, if not now. Douglas came out with their DC-8 a bit later than the 707 but found a market for this multi-option, change-this-change-that 4 turbojet aircraft. It carried 180 passengers at 935 kph as far as 11,270 km non-stop.

Douglas too

That old competitor Douglas - now McDonnell Douglas also brought out a twin, the DC 10-30. It goes on and on being improved. It can handle over 170 passengers also at nearly sonic speeds.

Russia Keeps Trying

Russia produced some good jet airliners, like the Ilyushin, but people from the west seldom flew in them.

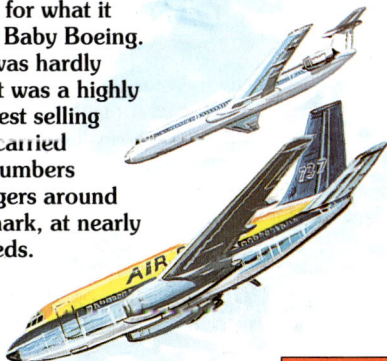

Some Baby!

In the mid '60s Boeing saw a slot for what it called the Baby Boeing. The 737 was hardly that, but it was a highly efficient best selling twin that carried variable numbers of passengers around the 130 mark, at nearly sonic speeds.

GOING FOR WIDTH

Wide Bodies

When Boeing brought out their 747 wide-bodied jet, people gaped. In 1970, its enormous size made it look dangerously slow as it approached to land. The 747 was soon nicknamed the Jumbo, which Boeing objected to at first. Its enormous cabin could carry over 500 passengers. It could cruise at close to 1,000 kph, for about 11,270 km. Some airports had trouble coping with the rush of passsengers all arriving at once, much more so when two Jumbos arrived at more or less the same time. The aircraft is hugely successful.

Europe Moves

Britain, through British Aerospace (BAe), is part of the European group, Airbus Industrie, building a range of very successful wide body jets. By sharing the tasks and costs it is possible to compete with the US giants. Britain's main task is to manufacture the high-tech wings which are shipped to Toulouse, France, for assembly. The A300 was the first twin-aisle, twin-engined airliner made. It started flying in 1974 and was unique for 10 years. Other manufacturers were worried.

Fly by Wire

The success of the Airbus range of aircraft meant that the firm grew to become today the second most important aircraft company in the world. There are five twins, the A320, A321, A310, A300 and A330 with different ranges and passenger numbers. The 320 has Fly By Wire (FBW) control. FBW means that when the pilot moves his cockpit controls, computers tell hydraulics how to move the flying surfaces - like ailerons and rudder. The computer does not allow the pilot to exceed the aircraft's limits. Some pilots have argued that in emergency that could be bad. But when the aircraft was announced, a record number of orders tumbled in.

All That Way

The first 4-engined Airbus, the A340, is newly in service. Its range is so amazingly long it can fly non-stop from London to Perth, Australia. Maximum cruising speed is Mach 0.86 - in the 970 kph area. The British-made wings can be used for two or four engined aircraft - never achieved before. All the Airbus models are quiet, safe, comfortable and economical, and the makers expect to hold 30% of the world market. The US industry is challenged.

More for the Rich
Jet engined, pressurised aircraft for busy and moneyed executives hustled into the market from the mid-'60s. Most are twins, with the engines set well back, presumably to keep them well away from the access door and for quietness in flight. A well known model is the Learjet which carries up to 8 passengers at the good speed of 885 kph.

Wingtip Tanks
The Israelies make the Westwind, 10 seats, which carries wingtip fuel tanks and has the astonishing range of over 5,320 km at Mach 0.8 - getting near the sound barrier.

The Exception
The Falcon 50, unusally, has three engines. It can carry up to 12 passengers for long, even trans-Atlantic distances at Mach 0.86. Dassault, of France, are the makers.

Gulfstream
The latest model from Gulfstream is very high tech indeed. It has tipped up wingtips (winglets) for less drag, a very advanced flightdeck and big enough fuel reserves to cover nearly 8,050 km. So, is it still a 'bizjet'? They say so.

THE MIGHTY MICRO

Angry Wasps

In the early '80s people on the ground began to notice tiny aircraft flying overhead and making a noise like a million angry wasps. The 'microlight' had arrived.

Flexwings ...

In some microlights you change direction simply by moving your bodyweight about - the big single wing overhead flexes obligingly.

Fixed Wings ...

There is a move towards fixed wing microlights which have the same controls as big aircraft - like the MW6.

... or Powerchute?

Recently an overhead parachute-like canopy has come to microlight flying. When the pilot revs up his engine, the parachute inflates, and airflow lifts it.

Trans-Atlantic

Dutchman Eppo Numan has flown the Atlantic in his flexwing microlight, brave if mad.

Flukey Winds

A sudden wind shift probably caused a DC10 to crash at Faro Airport, Portugal, killing more than 50 people and injuring hundreds more. A wing seems to have dropped on landing. This can happen from 'wind shear'. An aircraft depends on the flow of air over its wings, so if a headwind suddenly lulls or changes direction, it can cause loss of lift and an instant crash. New wind behaviour warning systems for pilots are being installed at major airports.

Hitting the High Ground

Most crashes, about five a year, happen when pilots in poor visibilty, and usually on the landing approach, fly into mountains or hilltops. Flight decks are fitted with Ground Proximity Warning Systems. If the ground is too close, a robot-like voice says, 'Pull up.' But the GPWS can only measure what is beneath, not what lies ahead though scientists are working on that.

Aircraft Collisions

Mid-air collisions are not common and many airliners carry a system to warn pilots if another aircraft is approaching dangerously. Near misses - 'airmisses' in aviation jargon - are more frequent and often involve a private pilot flying where he shouldn't be.

Black (Red) Boxes

For years so-called black boxes, which actually are red, and more correctly called Flight Data Recorders, have played vital roles in understanding air accidents. These crash resistant devices give accident investigators much information about the aircraft's speed, height, attitude, engine settings, and so on. Also, comments between the pilots, and between the control tower and the pilots are recorded for play-back.

Now in Pictures

Now the so-called Aircraft Data Analysis and Presentation System has been developed in Canada. This high-tech device can combine information taken from the black box with readings from the aircraft's instruments, and can add other information from radar stations and even eye witnesses, to give pictures of the incident. Investigators can even choose which angle they want to see - including from above. ADAAPS is being taken up by airlines.

Ground Control

Ground controllers in the 'tower' look directly at the aircraft as they 'push out' (moved by tractor), start up, taxy, pause at the holding point and eventually take off. The controller's permission is needed for every move. After take-off the captain radios, 'Thank you and goodbye,' to the tower and is handed to another controller who only sees the aircraft on his screen in the Air Traffic Control Centre.

Air Tunnels

Airspace over Britain is divided into two separately controlled Flight Information Regions (FIRs) known as London and Scottish. Aircraft must use invisible 'tunnels' or airways, and be kept at least five miles apart. On arrival they may have to circle in 'stacks' before landing. Sometimes after the landing approach has started the controller will order 'go around'. He is asking the plane to circle the runway before descending, to allow more time between aircraft touching down.

Look No Hands

Back in 1965, British scientists developed 'Autoland' to enable pilots to land in very poor visibility. The aircraft is locked onto a directional radio beam 16 km out from the airport, then onto a second glide path beam. In 1982, a Tristar aircraft landed in zero visibility at Heathrow using the system. Without it no aircraft is allowed to land unless the pilot can see the runway from a height of 61 m (200 ft). Regulations state that all parts of the system have to show a reliability of not more than one accident in 10 million landings - but the safety standard is much better at only one accident in 100 million landings.

Where Am I?

Early navigation was done by reading a 'mickey mouse' compass which pointed to magnetic north (not quite the same as true north), wobbled a lot and was often affected by other magnetic fields - like when the pilot thinks the needle is pointing north but it's pointing to his golf clubs. Then came beacons on the ground aircraft could lock onto - the VOR, for Very High Frequency Omni-directional Radio. But you can't have beacons in mid-ocean. Locking on to satellites is the answer.

Thanks Airbus

The brand new computer designed Boeing 777 is scheduled to fly in 1995. Boeing admitted they had felt the competition from the wide-bodied Airbus aircraft, and set about their own version, an even wider bodied jet twin. 'Making the 777 is a risk,' a Boeing spokesman said. 'It's a $4 billiion programme to make the newest, most advanced airliner.' They even had to build a new assembly plant for the project.

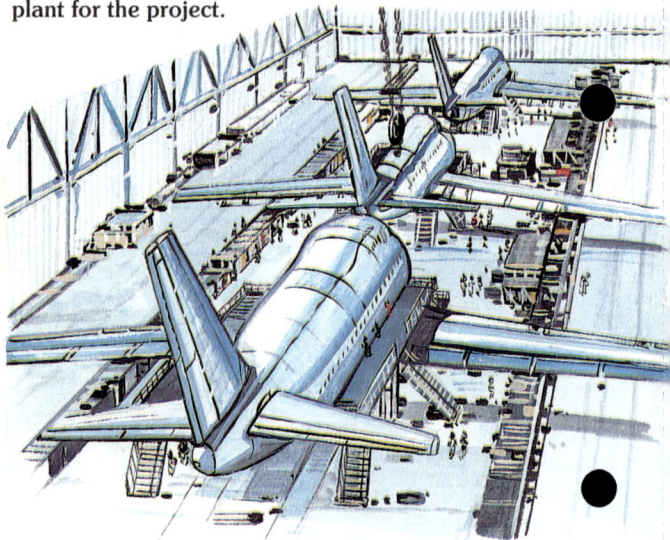

A feature of the 777 is that it has 'flex zones' meaning that seats, toilets and kitchen galleys can easily be made larger or smaller to suit the airlines. The aircraft will be put through a 40-year battering of simulated flight tests to ensure its strength. Boeing have adopted the 'fly-by-wire' control system. The 777 will be able to carry as many as 440 economy passengers with a maximum range of 9,020 km. Speed has yet to be revealed.

State of the Art

One day, a British engineer on a North Sea oil rig saw a sight that surprised him very much. An aircraft with a very strange triangular shape was flying high and refuelling from an escorting tanker. The engineer, who was an expert at aircraft recognition sketched it, and later showed it to *Janes* Defence Weekly.' At *Janes* they said it was probably the US's most top secret plane, the Aurora. This amazing aircraft can fly at eight times the speed of sound, 8,500 kph, and can climb to an almost incredible and near-airless height of 130,000 ft.

The aeroplane, known as Hypersonic, has no wings - its 75 degree triangular shape and massive liquid methane burning ramjet engines are enough. People living in Argyll, Scotland, have complained of hearing a pulsating, ear-splitting shriek, which further suggests the Aurora is flying over the Atlantic. It can reach any part of the world within three hours.

Ramjet Power

At over twice the speed of sound, Mach 2, no compressor is needed. The inward rush of air heated and allowed to blast out is enough to maintain mind numbing speeds.

Son of Concorde

Will there be a 'son'? Everyone admits that Concorde, now about 17 years old, was a very expensive project which would never have happened without the input of taxpayers' money. Yet interest in a second generation supersonic airliner remains intense. Today's Concorde burns four times the fuel of a jumbo, partly from having to slow down when the sonic boom would annoy people on the ground. Nasa scientists think they can reduce the boom to a 'rumble'. Other experts are doubtful. Certainly a new Concorde would have to be more fuel efficient and bigger, probably carrying 300 people. BAE and Aerospatiale, who built the old Concorde are well advanced with a study project. Other airlines, even including Boeing, are joining in. But some eminent environment experts think that super Concordes would devastate the upper atmosphere. Who's right?

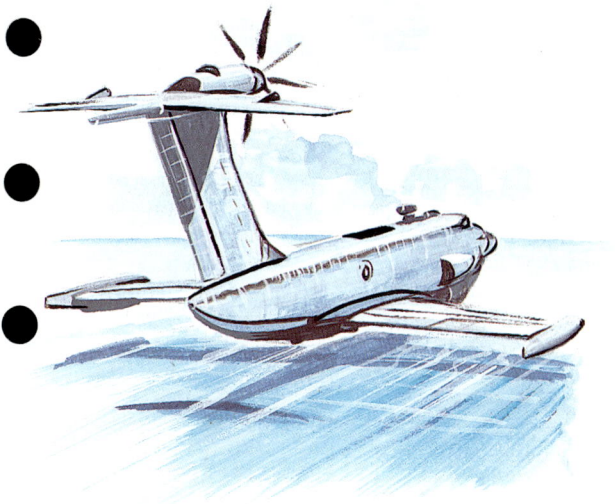

Riding a Cushion

For many years it has been known that aircraft flying low over water benefit from what is called 'ground effect'. The Russians went further than any other nation in studying this and are now making their findings known. As the aircraft flies low over the water surface the air is tightly compresed underneath. Fuel consumption is much reduced. The Russians have developed the 'Ekranoplan' from this, which combines 'skimming' with being able to hover for coming ashore, or to climb thousands of metres high. It is said the Ekranoplan could arrive with equal ease on a beach, or on top of the cliffs of Dover. The Russians predict fuel consumption down to only 20% of normal and very high speeds. Watch the ground effect plane!

Fly to the Office

About 10 years ago former Boeing engineer, Fred Barker, decided that the way to get through traffic was to fly over the top of it. Now he has produced the prototype of his car-like Sky Commuter. It is a two-passenger, Vertical Take-Off and Landing aircraft. Despite its smallness and strangeness, the Sky Commuter is technically very advanced. It has fly-by-wire control, and the body is made of Kevlar and graphite - Kevlar being eight times stronger than steel. The Sky Commuter has a gas turbine engine which drives alternators, which power electric motors - which turn the three fans to give lift. Its cruising speed is 135kph. You need a pilot's licence and a good head for heights - the machine can reach 10,000 ft!

Another Traffic Dodge

A cheaper and environmentally more friendly way to beat traffic jams has just been demonstrated by a Southampton University science lecturer. He developed and flew a man-powered airship 14.5m long and pedal powered. So far the craft has had only one known outing - a 10 km journey at 11 kph.

Cars to Planes Again

Honda, the Japanese motor manufacturers, are developing a jet aircraft with very advanced wings made from a compound carbon fibre material. The surprising venture is taking place in the US, and details of performance and cost have not been announced.

Superfast Helicopter

Coming soon is the X-wing helicopter. This will overcome the problem of the slowness of ordinary helicopters. The X-wing will take off with its overhead blades rotating in the normal way. When it has picked up speed, the blades, which are very large, will lock, shaped like an X, and under computer control will act like fixed wings. Now the helicopter becomes an aircraft, and jet engines will give it a cruising speed of over 1,120 kph. The X-wing may rival airliners on some routes. It is being developed by Sikorsky (see page 22), a main inventor and first manufacturer of helicopters.

Fighting Fatigue

Metal fatigue has always been a threat to the safety of aircraft. The Stealth fighter, and later Stealth bomber aircraft can defeat radar detection partly by their shape and partly by new materials used in their construction. Now an even more advanced material, 'Glare' has been developed. Glare stands for Glass Reinforced Composite, and is a mixture of glass, epoxy and aluminium. The makers say it will give a weight saving of 30% and will end the risk of metal fatigue. Passenger planes will use it.

Staggering Power

The weekly magazine The Engineer describes Rolls-Royce's new Trent engine as having a 'raw power that is staggering'. The engine has performed brilliantly under test which is just as well since it has cost £500 million to develop. Safety tests included throwing slabs of ice and dead chickens into the running engine - and it kept running. Boeing and Airbus, among others, are placing multi-million pound orders.

Airships Hang On

In the '30s airships looked set for a successful future until major crashes spoiled that. Recently, in the '80s, the age of airships seemed to be returning. A company named Airship Industries produced impressive and safe airships made of carbon fibre and plastics. Helium, also safe, was used for lift. But there are unsolved problems with airships, and the effort failed. These lighter than air craft are difficult to handle on the ground, and flying them unloaded means dumping expensive helium. But some are still in the air and in production. Hot air versions, burning propane for lift, look promising. And Zeppelin, the original airship makers are doing development work. All is not lost.

Will it, won't it?

McDonnel Douglas, once fierce rivals of Boeing, have been talking, a little vaguely, about their proposed new jumbo contender, the MD12. It is intended to compete in the jumbo market. But experts see nothing exciting in this big, 4-engined, orthodox aircraft, and some doubt if it will ever reach production. If it does it will have to be good to beat both Boeing and Airbus.

News - the Big One

The most exciting single piece of aviation news for ages is that there almost certainly will be a 'Super Jumbo' successor to today's 747s. But it will be years before it flies. Boeing and the European Airbus group, bitter rivals in airliner manufacturing and sales, surprised the world by becoming partners in a feasibility study to work out the design of the aircraft, and to look at the market. Estimates are that it will cost $5 billion to $10 billion to develop the new super jumbo - and only a dozen airlines would be big enough to buy it. Well, there are about a thousand parts in a single Boeing door! No single manufacturer could take on that cash risk - so the hatchet has been buried. The world's biggest airliner, which might be assembled in Britain, will carry 800 passengers at high but sub-sonic speeds.

Cockpits Today

Cockpits have changed. Instead of looking at flickering needles, pilots flying the new 777 watch six large display screens. Information will be shown on them by 'liquid crystal' figures and symbols which means they can be easily read even in sunlight, and are lightweight and cool. A big change from the Tiger Moth's low-tech cockpit!

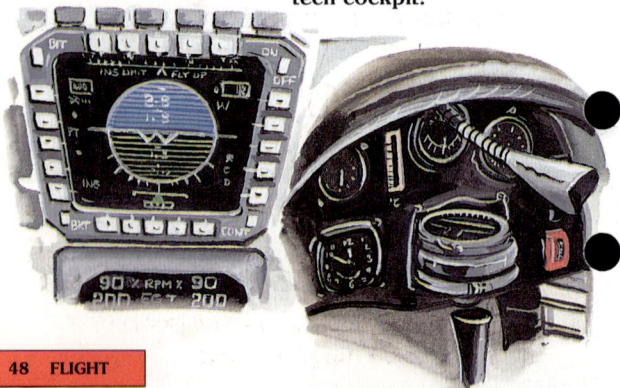